MILLIONS OF EELS

To the best of our knowledge, the life cycle contained in this book is accurate. However, the stages of the cycle that occur far out at sea cannot be confirmed.

First published 1991

Ashton Scholastic Limited
Private Bag 1, Penrose, Auckland 5, New Zealand.

Ashton Scholastic Pty Ltd
PO Box 579, Gosford, NSW 2250, Australia.

Scholastic Inc.
730 Broadway, New York, NY 10003, USA.

Scholastic Canada Ltd
123 Newkirk Rd, Richmond Hill, Ontario L4C 3G5, Canada.

Scholastic Publications Ltd
Marlborough House, Holly Walk, Leamington Spa, Warwickshire CV32 4LS, England.

ISBN 0-590-43954-5
Text copyright © 1989 by Howard Small.
Illustrations copyright © 1989 by Ulco Glimmerveen.
All rights reserved. Published by Scholastic Inc.,
730 Broadway, New York, NY 10003, by arrangement with
Ashton Scholastic Ltd.

12 11 10 9 8 7 6 5 4 3 2 1   1 2 3 4 5 6 / 9

Printed in Hong Kong
First Scholastic printing, May 1991

MILLIONS OF EELS

OF

by Howard Small
Illustrated by Ulco Glimmerveen

SCHOLASTIC INC.
New York   Toronto   London   Auckland   Sydney

Millions of eggs,
floating . . .

hatching.

Leaf-thin young,
drifting with the current.

4

Nearing the shore,
changing.

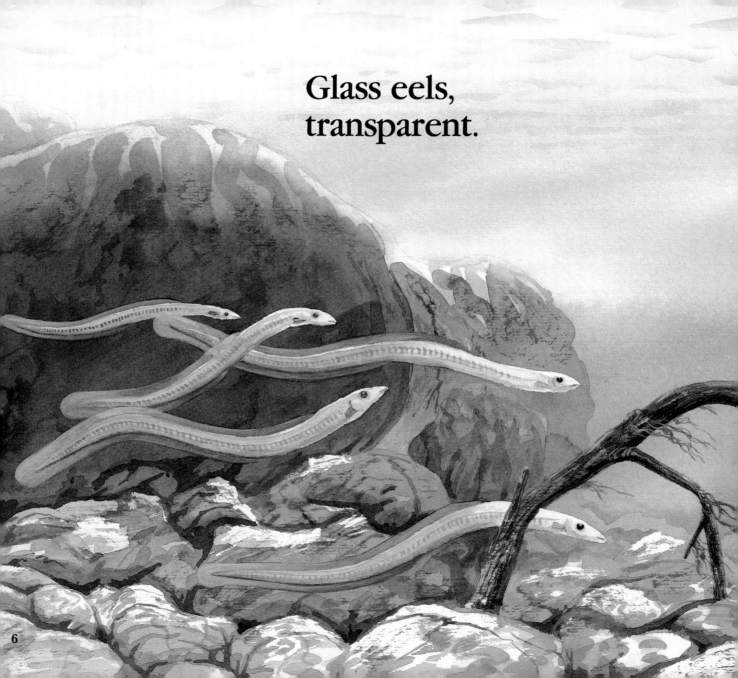

Glass eels,
transparent.

Growing darker,
becoming elvers.

Swimming upstream,
climbing waterfalls.

9

Drain and pipe travellers.

Wriggling, squeezing,
sliding through and under,

finding homes.

13

Hunting.

Ever-changing.

15

Yellowbellies,
slow and sluggish
during winter.

16

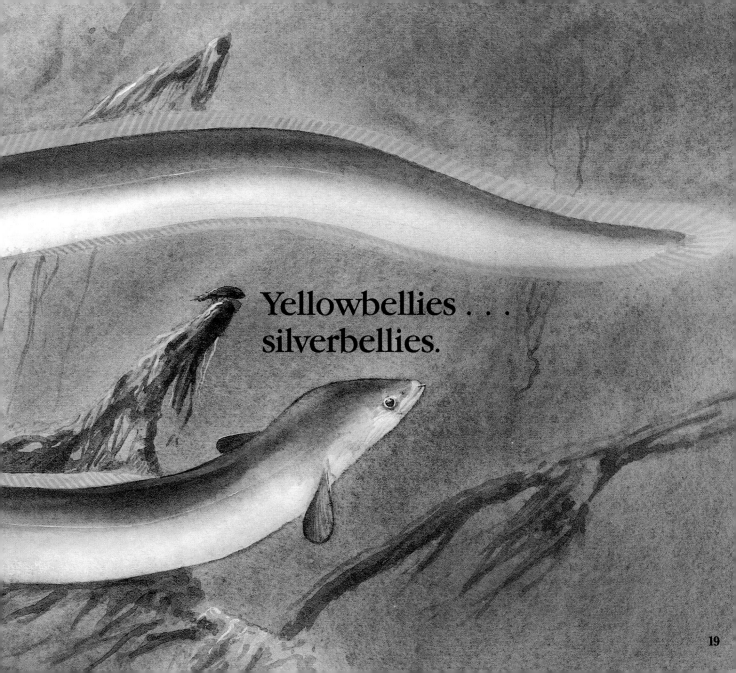

Yellowbellies . . .
silverbellies.

Escaping eel pots and fishermen,
returning to the open sea.

Breeding.

Millions of eggs,
floating . . .

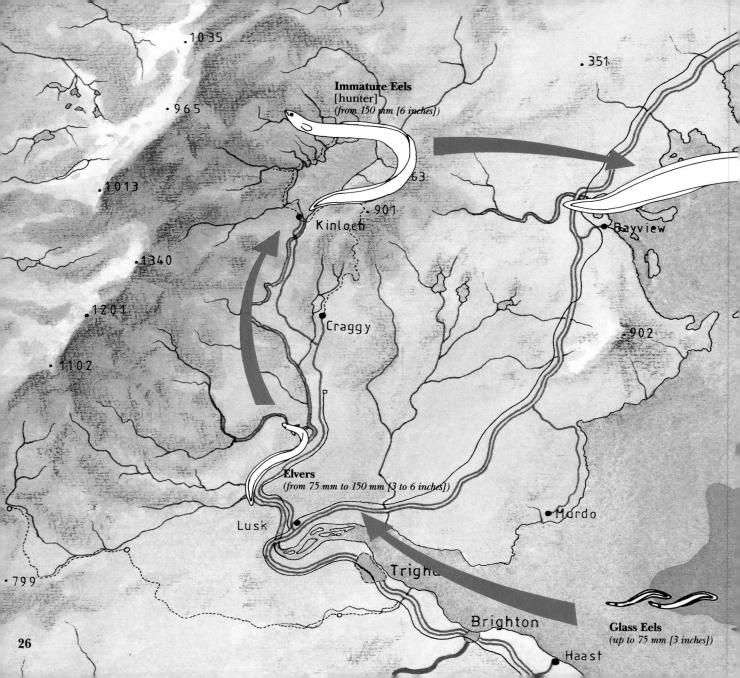

Immature Eels
[hunter]
(from 150 mm [6 inches])

Elvers
(from 75 mm to 150 mm [3 to 6 inches])

Glass Eels
(up to 75 mm [3 inches])

Kinloch

Craggy

Bayview

Lusk

Mordo

Trigham

Brighton

Haast

.1035

.965

.1013

.1340

.1201

.1102

.799

.351

.63

.901

.902

26

Clifton

200 METRES [656 FEET]

The Life Cycle of the Freshwater Eel

Publisher's Note: This map and the places on it have been invented to show the journey eels may take in their life cycle.

Migrating Adults
[yellowbellies — silverbellies]
(from 900 mm to 1800 mm [3 to 6 feet])

Spawning Adults
(from 900 mm to 1800 mm [3 to 6 feet])

Eggs
(up to 6 mm [0.24 inches])

Leptocephalus
[larvae]
(up to 60 mm [2.4 inches])

NB: Sizes indicated in parentheses are approximate only. 27

The Life Cycle of the Freshwater Eel

Egg — The eggs in this book are small cells that will hatch into young eels. Deep down in the sea, a female eel can lay up to 20 million eggs — more than any other fish!

Larva — The baby eels or larvae hatch from the eggs and float up to the surface, looking for food and sunlight. Baby eels are thin, about the thickness of a leaf and only a few centimetres (inches) in length. They are transparent or "see-through". The larvae slowly swim toward land in a trip that may take longer than a year.

Glass Eel — The eels start to shrink in appearance. Their thin bodies become rounder but they are still transparent so they are called glass eels.

Elver — The eels continue to shrink and their bodies become shorter and rounder. They also become darker in colour. We call this colouring pigmentation. Early in the springtime elvers swim into the rivers and sometimes find homes in the most unlikely places. (See pages 8-13.)

Yellow Eel — The eels continue to develop and to change colour. They become yellowish-green in colour. Sometimes yellow eels are called yellowbellies.

Silver Eel — When the eels are between five and twelve years in age, they are fully grown and ready to migrate. In the autumn (fall), the female eel puts on an extra layer of fat and stops eating. The sides of her skin become silvery in colour. She is a silver eel, able to breed. She swims with other females toward the sea where male eels join them. Together they will travel or migrate thousands of kilometres (miles) back to the ocean where, deep down in the sea, the eels' life cycle will begin again.